The New Green Smoothie Diet Solution

Nature's Fast Lane For Peak Health

Elizabeth Swann
www.Greensmoothies.me

Table of contents

Dedication

To my lovely daughters Sarah and Ruth and my amazing Husband Guy.

You are the reasons I wake up each morning with a smile on my face – I wonder where I would be without you.

And to all my clients at the "*Carmel Center For Holistic Therapies*" and "*Mount Carmel Hospital*" for inspiring me to write such a book.

Welcome to the Wonderful World of Green Smoothies!

If you are anything like me, then I am going to assume that (like me), you want to look great and feel great! Perhaps you have tried all the fad diets, "magic" supplements, detox programs and the million and one other products and programs that are available today. I would be willing to bet that none of them worked (they didn't work for me); to help you lose weight, feel more energetic or improve your mood and reduce your stress. I have discovered that there is a very good reason for that!

There is absolutely no fad diet, detox, or magic supplement that can change habits that are inherently unhealthy!

Your health and well-being depend on your diet. Wrong food choices can affect your weight, your energy levels, your immunity to disease, stress, digestive system disorders and just about everything else to do with good health. Your diet is also in control of the condition of your skin and hair; no amount of fancy hair potions and lotions can help you if your diet is lacking in the essential nutrients required for healthy skin and hair. I should know; I tried them all!

Thing is; it is really easy to make the right choices!

You have a whole new outlook on life is when you feel great and look great. The easiest, most convenient way I know of to get there is with green smoothies. *Green Smoothies can literally change your life! They certainly changed mine!* I am now de-stressed, detoxed and slimmer than I've been in years. I have not had a cold in 5 years, so I know that the immune boosting properties of green smoothies are the real thing. I have boundless energy; I feel like a kid again!

A healthy diet does not mean eating only certain foods or eating on a strict schedule; it is about getting the maximum amount of nutrition, in the most delicious way possible. You do not need to be a vegetarian or adhere to any far-out dogmas or programs. Simple healthy nutrition is at your fingertips right here in this book.

I have worked long and hard to come up with a way to look and feel better that does not take up a lot of time, or involve major preparation and messy clean-ups. I have to say green smoothies are it!

I was determined to come up with a solution to my weight gain and flagging energy. I was familiar with the concept of "Green Smoothies" and I was aware that they were very popular with some people. So, of course, I decided to try one.

One green smoothie led to another, and here we are! I have never felt better in my life! I am losing those pounds I accumulated over these last few years, I no longer have heartburn and indigestion all the time, I have lots of energy and my skin and hair are looking healthy again. I actually crave food that is healthy rather than sweets and snacks.

There are, however, some misconceptions about what the term "Green Smoothie" means. Green smoothies are not about glasses full of nasty tasting greens, that you would never be caught dead eating, because you cannot stand the way they taste. It is about incorporating those same super food greens into tasty delicious smoothies that boost your health and taste great at the same time. In a smoothie that is made properly, *you will never even know you have eaten those greens*, except for the green color of the smoothie.

You do not have to survive on a *"Green Smoothie Diet"* either. The way to use green smoothies for optimal health is by substituting a smoothie for one meal a day, or having one for a snack instead of packaged food. Green smoothies are filling, as well as healthy, and your body will thank you for it; I know mine does. Once those pesky issues, such as a few extra pounds, a lack of energy and the stress start to disappear, you will be amazed at how easy it actually was to achieve results. These results will last, too; if you just keep on doing things the green smoothie way.

If you are still hesitant, just give one a try and see if you don't begin to see green smoothies in a whole new light. I certainly did as soon as I tried them.

My Green Smoothie Story

I have always believed that there is a deep connection between the foods we eat, and the way we feel. In my early twenties I was severely overweight, depressed and cranky most of the time. To be quite honest, I was all of the above most of my childhood, and teen years as well.

When I was in college I was so tired all of the time, I missed most of my classes and eventually flunked out my first year. I was suffering from high cholesterol, obesity, and had the attention span of a bumble bee. Trying to effectively cope with the pressures of exams and life in general I turned to sweet, salty and fried comfort foods to escape from it all.

I knew I wasn't making the best decisions, but the emotional connection to food was just too hard to break at the time. It soon became a vicious circle from which I could not, and did not want to escape from. I think they call that depression these days, which only leads to more of the same.

At this point in my life I was at a crossroads where I had the choice to either keep on living the way I was (overweight, tired and not happy with my body), or get an entirely new life plan! I was about to get married to my wonderful husband, and I decided that my marriage would symbolize a whole series of new beginnings.

I thought, "What better way to get healthier than become an expert in all-natural therapies?" So, I enrolled in a 4 year curriculum to become a licensed naturopath. Over the course of those 4 years I learned all about the human body, and how to heal it using natural approaches that treat problems from the root and not only the symptoms.

The more I learned, the healthier I became. I cut out dairy products, gluten and processed foods almost completely from my diet, and started eating more fruits, vegetables and whole foods. I couldn't believe how much stronger and better I felt physically. The emotional payoffs were even more amazing than that! I lost all of my "baby fat" and even started going to yoga and meditation classes.

When I started treating others in my private practice, I discovered that many women, and even men, felt exactly the same way as I had felt my whole life. They were trying to live the best way they could, but there were too many nutritional "roadblocks" that were standing in the way of better health. Being able to learn more about how people related to food, has taught me even more about how our food choices affect all aspects of our lives.

The Green Smoothie Connection

I discovered the power of eating greens early on in my studies as a Naturopath, but never tried blending them together with fruits! When I tasted my first smoothie I was amazed how tasty and refreshing it was. So I started drinking them on a regular basis. After 2 weeks of drinking a shake a day I was feeling a lot more energized, relaxed and stronger. I've never stopped since!

I started prescribing green smoothies to my clients, and was completely amazed by the results. They were not only fast and easy to make, they were also proving to be a very powerful healing tool that I could use to help people feel better and improve their own lives.

Green smoothies aren't a miracle magic pill, and they won't heal every disease in the world, but they are extremely powerful as a method to provide your body with a quick and easy boost of high level nutrients. The energy and the health benefits are simply amazing, especially when you can get all of this from a simple green smoothie!

Greens Taste Good?

I was never a fan of greens, and maybe you aren't either. And that's exactly where green smoothies come into play. They provide an amazingly tasty way to consume large amounts of greens, without feeling like you're eating an entire forest. With a few little tweaks, even the least adventurous among us can find creative ways to ramp up the taste, while keeping all the benefits of a green smoothie.

Green smoothies are also a great way to introduce a variety of different greens to the younger, more food fussy generation. My daughters love having their special green "Milkshakes" as we like to call them at home.

I want to end with an ancient Buddhist saying – *"A journey of 1,000 miles begins with a single step"*.

I hope this book will help you take the first step to a stronger and healthier you. Just remember to take it slow and you'll reap the benefits of drinking green smoothies a lot faster than you think.

I am honored to be able to share my findings and experiences with you in this book. Thanks for reading, and I wish you a wonderful and refreshing journey into the world of green smoothies!

A Quick Breakdown
Of The Books Contents

This is a handy reference that will help you find exactly what you are looking for.

Chapter 1- Why Go Green-Smoothies? covers the amazing benefits of greens and why you should include them in your diet and start drinking delicious Green Smoothies.

Chapter 2 – Perfect Smoothies Every Time! will show you how to become a smoothie making expert in no time! Tips and tricks are included to help you create the perfect smoothie every time, and how to make sure it appeals to your taste buds.

Chapter 3 – Detoxifying Your Life is all about detoxifying; why we detoxify, and the health benefits we can expect from detoxifying. Great tasting detoxifying green smoothie recipes are included.

Chapter 4–Lose Weight will teach you the fastest and healthiest ways to lose weight using green smoothies. You'll learn how to break free from all of those old weight loss myths that have had you trapped in a nightmare for years. You will also learn how to achieve amazing results with the great tasting recipes for delicious smoothies that will supercharge your weight loss goals.

Chapter 5–De-Stress reduce the negative effects of stress on your life. Learn how to de-stress and relax a little. You won't believe how easy it is with the right nutrients and activities.

Chapter 6 – Energize & Revitalize is where you learn how to dramatically boost your energy levels so you feel younger and stronger. Find out what zaps all of your energy and how to get it back now!

Chapter 7–Mood Boosting you CAN feel as good as you look. Find out how green vegetable and fruit smoothies can improve your whole outlook on life.

Chapter 8 – Strengthen Your Immune System offers important tips on boosting your immune system. Learn how to boost your resistance to colds and flu. Find out how to increase your body's ability to fight off infection and disease, simply by have one of these tasty green smoothies every day!

Chapter 9 – Healthy Hair & Skin shows you how to improve the condition of your skin and hair by altering your nutritional habits.

Chapter 10 – Smoothie Master Class customize and personalize your green smoothies with advanced tips and tricks

Chapter 11 – Best Blender Purchasing Tips this chapter will show you exactly what you need to look for when purchasing a blender and how to get the best results using it. You don't need a $500 blender to get good results! I will cover the basics so you can make the best decision possible.

Chapter 12 – Taking The Next Step contains easy tips to help you improve your health. Find out how minor changes in your diet can make all the difference in the way you look and feel.

Chapter 13–Green Smoothie FAQ's over the years I've been asked many questions about the do's and don't of drinking green smoothies. In this chapter I answer some of the most burning questions.

The Recipes – Throughout the book you will find different recipes that correspond to specific categories. For quick reference to any of the recipes, find them on the table of contents. If you're reading the digital version of this book, simply click on the recipe you want to prepare on the table of contents and you'll be sent to the corresponding page!

Why Green Smoothies?

Most of us know that leafy green vegetables are good for us. What many of us do not realize, is that greens contain almost all of the nutrients that the human body requires. Of course, you get different amounts of these nutrients from each green and you should eat a variety to gain the full benefits of greens.

The major reason why greens are less popular than other vegetables is their somewhat bitter flavor. That makes Green Smoothies a sensible alternative. When mixed in with fruits, the bitter taste of greens just seems to magically disappear.

The biggest advantage to drinking Green Smoothies, is that even if you eat greens whole, they are filled with cellulose and hard for the body to break down to retrieve the nutrients. When you liquefy them in a smoothie, your body has easier access to these nutrients.

Greens give you healthy doses of *Vitamin K* that helps the body produce proteins for bone health. Deficiencies in this vitamin are related to birth defects and cancer. Greens are one of the very few foods that contain Vitamin K. They are also full of Vitamins A, C, E and many of the B vitamins, minerals and phytonutrients.

They are also a source of protein and amino acids, which are protein building blocks. Ingesting your amino acids in this way, allows the body to create the right proteins, as opposed to the complex proteins contained in meat, which forces the body to work harder to break them down for proper digestion. Greens contain enzymes vital to proper digestion without flatulence. This makes them a perfect food to combine in Green Smoothies or any vegetable recipe.

Remember that organic is best, but always use fresh greens. Once they start to wilt, they begin to lose their nutrients. Greens contain large amounts of cellulose which makes them hard to chew and digest properly. By using them in Green Smoothies, the blender does all the work of releasing those nutrients and making them available to your body. It also helps if you chop them up first and add them to your smoothie as the last ingredient.

Here are some of the greens that are commonly chosen for Green Smoothies and their nutritional information.

1. **Baby Spinach** is an excellent starter green because the flavor is so mild. It is packed with *iron, fiber, protein, calcium and Vitamins A, B9, C, E and K.*

2. **Kale** also has a fairly mild flavor and provides *water, fiber, protein, Vitamins A, K, B1, B2, B3, B5, B9, B12, C, D, E, calcium, iron, magnesium, potassium, phosphorus and manganese.*

3. **Parsley** is a mildly flavored herb that gives you *fiber, protein, VitaminsB1, B2, B3, B55, B6, B9, C, K, calcium, iron, magnesium, phosphorus, potassium and zinc.*

4. **Bok Choy** is also known as Chinese Cabbage and it has a succulent flavor that many people enjoy. It contains nutrients such as *fiber, protein calcium, iron, magnesium and Vitamins A and C.*

5. **Collard Greens** are related to broccoli and cabbage. They provide *protein, calcium, fiber and Vitamins A, C and K.*

6. **Dandelion Greens** are very popular with people and are used to make many foods and drinks. They contain super nutritional

properties including; *water, fiber, protein, Vitamins A, B1, B2, B3, B5, B6, B9, C, D, E, K, choline, calcium, iron, magnesium, manganese, phosphorus, potassium and zinc.*

7. **Romaine Lettuce** is mildly flavored and delicious, as well as nutritious. It contains *water, fiber, protein, Vitamins A, B9 and C, calcium, iron, phosphorus and potassium.*

8. **Cilantro** is actually the herb coriander and has a citrusy flavor. It provides *fiber, protein and Vitamins A and C.*

9. **Mustard Greens** have a stronger flavor than some greens. They contain *fiber, selenium, chromium, iron and zinc.*

These are only a few of the many greens that you can choose from. Believe it, the list would be very long, and it is up to you to choose the ones that you prefer. It is best to start out your Green smoothie adventure with the greens that have the milder flavors. It won't be such a shock to your taste buds and you can change them up once you have discovered how truly tasty Green Smoothies are!

Greens also provide serious antioxidants and are believed to help prevent cancer and heart disease.

Start with just a handful or two of greens and increase the amount gradually, as you get used to drinking green smoothies. As your taste buds adjust to the greens, you should shoot for working your way to at least ***3 cups of chopped greens per day***. Although all green vegetables are good for you, greens do not contain all the starch that is found in other green vegetables, therefore greens make better smoothies, with a better texture.

IMPORTANT INFORMATION: Certain greens, specifically those in the brassica family such as, kale, cabbage and turnips contain glucosinates, spinach and beet greens contain oxalic acid; both of which are mild toxins that the plant contains naturally. They are a natural defense against being eaten to extinction in the wild. However, they are harmless and may even provide some healthy benefits to humans, unless con sumed in large quantities. 2 bunches a day of any of them is perfectly safe, but it is not recommended to use the same greens all the time, day in and day out.

Try to use at least 7 varieties of greens per week. This gives you a wider range of ingredients to choose from and insures that you get all of the nutrition that greens have to offer. So, just rotate your greens, and make sure your rotation is from plant family to plant family, rather than within the same family!

Now we know all about greens and why we should choose them.

Perfect Smoothies Every Time!

Get ready, get set, and let's make some smoothies!

Even if you have never made smoothies before, you will soon be a master smoothie maker. Nothing is easier or simpler to prepare than a healthy green smoothie. Once you get started, you will be an expert in no time. There is no need to get bored with smoothie recipes, because soon you will be creating your own. Don't forget to refer to the tips on ingredients and additions in Chapter 10 for truly unique combinations that you will love!

Yes, I know, anyone can toss things into the blender and turn it on! However, there are techniques to getting the perfect consistency, the ideal texture and obtaining the proper temperature to create a satisfying smoothie experience. You can make smoothies all day, but if they are too thick, too thin, not smooth enough or not cold enough, they will not appeal to your taste buds. There really is an art to making the perfect thick and creamy smoothie.

There are really only 8 STEPS to the perfect Green Smoothie.

1. **Liquid** – There is normally some type of liquid ingredient added to every smoothie, and unless the recipe specifies otherwise, the liquid should be added first.

2. **Base** – The base is always fruit. Fruits are what give a smoothie its creamy texture and add the sweetness that makes it delicious. All fruits are not suitable to use for a base, water based fruits will make the mixture thin and runny. Refer to the list below to choose your base. Fruits should be added next.

3. **Mix your Flavors** – Using your favorite flavor fruits will only enhance your smoothie experience. Try to use fruit that has a strong flavor and whose flavor will be complementary to the base fruit that you used. It is okay to use more than one; the more fruit, the more nutrients your smoothie contains. It's all a matter of your taste preference, when you are making your own smoothie.

4. **Extra Ingredients** such as flax seeds, Chia Seeds, other super foods, spices, extracts, etc. should be added now.

5. **Pulse** several times to mix the base ingredients.

6. **Time to Add Those Greens** – Greens are what make a smoothie super nutritious, so add as many as you can. To achieve the maximum amount of health benefits from a smoothie, greens are the most essential ingredient. You should use about 40% greens with 60% fruit for the best taste. You can increase the ratio of greens as high as you want, as your taste buds adjust to having the greens in your smoothie. You will know you are getting the very best in nutrition when you have reached a level of 70% greens in your smoothies. Don't worry about what the greens will do to the taste of your smoothie, because the fruit is the key to totally disguising the taste of the greens.

7. **Blend** on high 30 seconds or until you achieve the desired result. (Some of those fancy expensive blenders have smoothie settings…hmmmm!)

8. **Pour your smoothie into a tall glass and enjoy!**

The only kitchen supplies you need to make smoothies are, of course, a blender, a chopping board and a sharp knife. The smaller you chop pieces of fruit and greens, the better the end result will be. This is especially true if you are not using a special high-powered blender.

Remove the core from fruits such as pineapple, for a smoother texture, (nobody likes lumps in their smoothie!) However, on the other hand, do not continue to blend any longer than necessary to achieve the desired consistency. The longer vegetables and fruit are exposed to the air, the more oxidation occurs (loss of nutrients).

Here are the liquids that work best in smoothies.

Water – Always use filtered, distilled or other bottled water that does not contain the chemicals that are found in tap water, or use crushed ice.

Green Tea – Loaded with antioxidants, just make it 2 to 4 times as strong as you would for drinking, and use it for your liquid or freeze it into ice cubes.

Coconut Water – Take a whole coconut and tap and drain the water for your smoothie liquid. While you are at it, the meat of the coconut is also an excellent addition for one of your fruit choices, especially when you are using other tropical fruits. Coconut water can also be purchased separately from the fruit. Just make sure that it has no added ingredients that you do not want.

Canned Fruit Nectar – There are many varieties of nectar at your local grocer. Choose from, coconut, agave, peach, strawberry and others. They are usually sweeter than juice, so use them wisely.

Fruit Juice – The fool-proof way to get the best juice is to make your own from fresh fruit, so squeeze it yourself whenever possible. You can use all-natural unsweetened fruit juice. It is even better if it is organic, unprocessed and unpasteurized. That way you get all the natural vitamins, antioxidants and enzymes that are processed right out of regular packaged fruit juice.

Here are the best fruits to use as a base so that you get that highly desirable creamy texture.

Banana – This is the number 1 choice for a base. The soft creamy texture of the banana's flesh converts perfectly into a smooth mixture.

Mango – If you want a tropical flavor, mango is the go-to fruit.

Peach – Naturally adds a sweeter flavor along with good texture.

Pear – This is another good choice if you like a sweet smoothie with a mild flavor.

Apple – If you like it sweet, or if you like it tart, you can find a perfect apple for either.

Papaya – This is another good tropical choice. Try mixing it half and half with mango!

For mixing the flavors, just choose your favorite fruits!

The fruits listed above are great for the base, because the majority of other fruits naturally contain more water content. If you add too much of the water fruits, your smoothie will be thin and watery. The perfect ratio of fruit should be one half as much flavoring (water) fruit as base. *Example: 2 bananas and 1 cup of strawberries.* It is best to add your flavor fruit a little at a time, and stop when you reach the consistency that you prefer.

Use any greens that you prefer.

Of course, there are many greens to choose from, so pick your greens according to your nutritional needs, and don't worry about how they taste, because you won't be able to taste them by the time you have added all the other ingredients! However, even though just about any green will do, it is best to rotate at least *7 different greens* in your smoothies each week to gain the full benefits of the nutrients they offer.

That's how you get all the healthy benefits that Green Smoothies have to offer!

What Do I Do If…?

My smoothie is too sweet – Add some extra greens, a stalk of celery or some sea salt to cut the sweetness.

It's not cold enough – Bananas and berries in particular can be frozen fresh and whole (do not peel bananas prior to freezing). Frozen ingredients make a much colder smoothie. You can also use ice in place of some of the liquid. (Always crush ice before adding it to the blender.)

It tastes bitter – Adding additional fruit will take care of this problem. Bananas, pineapple, ripe berries and sweet oranges work best.

It is just not sweet enough – You can always add sweetener to your recipe. Honey is ideal, as is agave nectar. You can also use sweeteners like Stevia or Splenda. Chopped dates or extra banana will work, as well. *Remember, the riper the fruit you use, the sweeter your smoothie will be!*

I can't get it thick enough – Try adding ¼ Avocado or a comparable amount of coconut meat. Both of these ingredients add a few calories, but they provide some of the "good" fats that are needed in your diet. The Avocado adds an extra creamy element to any smoothie. Additional greens can also help to thicken a smoothie.

How to Store Your Blended Smoothie

Smoothies are really not a *"prepare in advance"* food. They are at their very best taste, consistency and nutrition level when consumed immediately after preparation. The vitamins and other nutrients begin to oxidize and lose their potency very quickly once they have been exposed to the air.

However, if you have to store them temporarily, or you have leftovers, place them in an airtight container in the refrigerator. It will keep reasonably well overnight or for a few hours between breakfast and lunch.

When you are ready to have your stored smoothie, first shake it well, or give it another short spin in the blender. While it is sitting, the fruit fiber and liquids will tend to separate and should be thoroughly remixed before you drink it.

Tip – Never keep a smoothie longer than 24 hours; just discard it and make another.

Now that you know how to make the perfect smoothie it's time to try some!

For the recipes in this book, we will be using combinations of fruits and greens that are commonly available in the U.S. at farmer's markets and local grocery stores. There are many interesting and exotic fruits and vegetables that you can use, if you like them, and they can be obtained in your area.

Berry Broccoli Green Smoothie

Blueberries and broccoli make a surprisingly sweet and filling green smoothie.

    1 Banana, frozen and peeled
    ½ cup Blueberries, frozen
    1 cup Broccoli Spears, frozen
    ½ cup Water or Crushed Ice

Place all ingredients in the blender and puree until smooth.
Makes 1 Serving

Nutrition: This one has the ability to slow the progression of degenerative diseases. It is low in calories and filled with fiber, vitamins and antioxidants.

Rockstar Green Smoothie

Sweet cantaloupe makes this a tasty combo!

    3 cups Cantaloupe chilled, peeled, seeded and chopped
    2 handfuls Greens (large handfuls chopped)
    Blend ingredients on high until smooth.

Makes 2 Servings

Nutrition: Cantaloupe is also known as Rockmelon. It is sweet, contains Vitamins C & A, and has plenty of antioxidants and fiber. Spinach also provides fiber and vitamins plus iron. This one is low calorie, great for blood sugar and dieting.

CONGRATULATIONS! Now that we have mastered Green Smoothie making, let's move on and find out specific ways to use green smoothies to take our physical and mental health to a whole new level!

In Chapter 3 we will discuss using Green Smoothies to detox the body.

Detoxifying Your Life

Detoxifying your body occasionally gives you whole system a jolt of new energy. It cleans the digestive system, relieves common problems, such as indigestion, flatulence, constipation, and can even ease the symptoms of acid reflux disease. Detoxing also gives your immune system a huge boost and can jump start that weight loss regimen. It cleanses the blood and flushes the liver and kidneys. Detoxifying in a healthy way is good for your entire system.

The recommended schedule for detoxing is 4 times per year for a continuous 4 day period. It is easy when you make it a seasonal event, and then you can forget it. Performing a detox on a regular schedule also makes if far easier to stick to your healthy diet plan the rest of the time. Some like to do a one day detox if they feel the need, especially following holidays or other events when the tendency to eat a little too much of the *"not so good stuff"* is most overpowering.

The foods that you use when detoxifying, are the same ones, when assembled in different combinations that are good for you all the time!

What all this means, is that once you get started using green smoothies for optimum health benefits, detoxifying will actually seldom be necessary.

Which Foods are best for Detoxifying?

The main ingredients in any detoxifying green smoothie are **Fruit and Greens**. Fruit is chock-full of vitamins, antioxidants, phytonutrients, minerals and fiber. Loaded with water, fruit is the most powerful food for cleansing and detoxifying. Greens contain the super power of fiber, which is the natural cleanser of the body. Fiber keeps your digestive system running smoothly, and as clean as a whistle.

Of course, the fruit you use needs to be fresh and ripe. Fruit juice cannot be substituted for fruit in a detox smoothie, because the whole fruit is what contains all the fiber that helps to cleanse the body. As an ingredient in detoxing green smoothies, berries are fine, but you will have to eat a lot more of them than you would other fruit, because their fiber content is much lower. Calories and carbohydrates power the body up for a detox, and berries do not contain as much of either as other fruits.

Five Star Detoxifying Fruits: Citrus fruits; lemons, limes, grapefruits and oranges. These fruits have the most water content for flushing out toxins, and are the best fiber source for scrubbing out the digestive system. Next is pineapple, which contains the enzyme bromelain, which aids in digesting protein.

The Best Detox Greens: Parsley has long been used as a natural detox agent in many cultures. Use parsley all year for natural detox maintenance. Dandelion greens offer powerful cleansing properties. Kale contains a phytonutrient believed to prevent many diseases. Romaine lettuce is another good choice since it adds fiber as well as its water content to the mix.

Some healthy fats are also needed by the body during a detox, but they should comprise only 10 or 15% of your calorie intake while detoxing. These fats should come from sources such as small amounts of nuts, coconut, avocados and seeds added to some of your detox smoothies.

Keep these Tips in Mind When You Detoxify

1. ***Try to use only organic or farm fresh foods.*** It really kind of defeats the whole purpose of detoxifying, if the foods you use in your recipes contain chemicals and preservatives.

2. ***Always use whole fruits and vegetables.*** Eliminate processed foods from your diet every day, whether you are detoxing or not.

3. ***Drink lots of water.*** We have all heard this one a million times, but it is ***"so true."*** The majority of your body is water, and water is a major ingredient in your green smoothie detox recipes. It is what helps to get the job done.

4. ***Get enough sleep.*** Another one that has been drilled into us since the day we were born, but it really does take 7 or 8 hours of sleep every night for your body to renew itself and maintain your health.

5. ***Exercise.*** Here we go again, and what can I say; it is just simply true. Some form of exercise is vital to good health.

Detoxifying Green Smoothie Recipes

Keep in mind that citrus fruit is tart and can be rather sour. With the addition of greens these smoothies can also be slightly bitter. You may want to trade grapefruit for orange which is sweeter. You can also add a banana or some honey, Stevia or Splenda to adjust the taste to suit you.

Lemon Green Detox Smoothie

Love that citrusy-sweet Vitamin C, have this one instead of your morning OJ!

> ½ each Lemon and Lime, peeled and seeded
> 1 large Orange, juiced
> 2 Bananas, frozen and peeled
> 1 or 2 cups Dandelion Greens or Kale

Place all ingredients in blender. Process on high until mixture is smooth.
Makes 1 Serving

Nutrition: 316 calories, 2 grams fat, 6.7 grams protein, 79 grams carbs. Rich in: calcium, iron, potassium, magnesium and Vitamins C, E, K and B.

Grapefruit & Strawberry Detox Smoothie

This is a tart, yet sweet smoothie that is very refreshing.
>   1 cup Strawberries, fresh or frozen
>   1 Pink Grapefruit, peeled and seeded
>   1Banana, frozen and peeled
>   2 to 3 cups Romaine Lettuce, chopped

Pulse all ingredients except lettuce until mixed. Add lettuce and blend on high until creamy,
Makes 1 Serving

Nutrition: 345 calories, 2 grams fat, 11 grams protein, 80 grams carbs, Rich in: calcium, iron, Vitamins K, B1 & B6 and potassium.

Invigorating Detox Smoothie

The watermelon makes for a sweet and refreshing addition to your smoothie detox program.
>   2 cups Watermelon, chopped and seeded
>   1 Banana, frozen and peeled
>   1 Orange, peeled and seeded
>   1 Carrot, chopped
>   3 cups Kale, chopped
>   ½ cup Water or Crushed Ice

Combine all ingredients except greens in the blender and pulse until smooth. Add greens and blend on high to desired consistency is reached.
Makes 1 Serving

Nutrition: 391 calories, 2 grams fat, 11 grams protein, 95 grams carbs, 13.1 grams fiber, calcium, iron, Vitamins A, C, B1, B6 and K, magnesium and potassium.

Dandy Pineapple Detox Smoothie

This one is as potent as it is delicious, and it's filled with protein digesting enzymes from pineapple.

> 2 cups Pineapple, peeled, cored, cubed
> 1 Pear or Apple, peeled, cored, seeded, chopped
> 3 cups Dandelion Greens, chopped
> 1 cup Parsley, chopped
> ½ cup Water or Crushed Ice

Pulse all ingredients except greens in blender until mixed well. Add Greens and blend on high until creamy.
Makes 1 Serving

Nutrition: 364 calories, 2 grams fat, 8 grams protein, 89 grams carbs, 17.9 grams fiber, calcium, iron, Vitamins A, C, B1, B6 and K, magnesium, copper, phosphorous and potassium.

Parsley & Avocado Cleansing Smoothie

Creamy and sweet, it's hard to tell this one is healthy by the taste!

> 1 cup Parsley, fresh and chopped ¼ large Avocado, peeled and pitted 1 large Pear, peeled and cored 1 tbsp. Honey ¾ cup Water or Crushed Ice

Combine all ingredients in blender and process on high until smooth and creamy. To thin the mixture add water, to thicken it add additional ice.
Makes 1 Serving

Nutrition: 200 calories, rich in antioxidants, anti-inflammatories from honey and healthy fats from avocado.

In this chapter we have become professional *"**Detox Divas**"* by discovering the best ways and means for detoxification for life and health, including:

How, when, where and why to detox

1. The best fruits and vegetables for a successful detox regimen, and why we should use those specific food sources

2. A few extra tips to help our detox along

3. 6 delicious detox recipes that will definitely get us off to the right start!

WARNING: If at any time during a detox, you experience symptoms of hypoglycemia, hyperglycemia or suddenly rising and falling blood sugar levels, you should stop the detoxification process immediately and contact your physician.

In this chapter we learned all about using green smoothies to detoxify our bodies and found some great green smoothie recipes!

Let's move on to Chapter 4 and find out all about Green Smoothies For Rapid Weight Loss.

Easiest Weight Loss Method Ever

*L*et's be honest with one another; what could possibly be worse than going on yet another diet?

Take me, for example: When I passed the age of 40, I began to gain weight. I could not understand why! I didn't eat any differently than I ever had, and I had always been one of those people who are just naturally slim, no matter what they do. Well, believe me, once menopause began the "slim and trim me" was soon a thing of the past! My weight gain began around the abdomen, upper arms and face, and before I knew it I had gained almost 60 pounds.

In the last 5 years I have tried everything (***and I do mean everything!***) to lose the weight I gained. I just could not believe that I would never see that slim, shapely me again. Since I discovered the Green Smoothie, I am well on my way to getting back to the weight where I want and need to be. I truly believe that incorporating Green Smoothies into an otherwise sensible diet can help anyone to lose weight and keep it off forever! It certainly works for me.

One of the biggest fears we have when contemplating weight loss, is the dread associated with being deprived of our favorite foods and the sweets that we tend to crave. That fear drives us to cheat on ourselves.

We think: "oh a little of this won't hurt, and while we're at it, let's have a little of that too!". Before we know it, we are right back where we started, and then the frustration with the whole idea of dieting sets in again. The remarks below sum up how most people feel about diets:

1. *Almost everyone wants to lose some or a lot of weight.*

2. *Most of us have tried multiple diet programs that failed.*

3. *Even if it worked temporarily, soon we're right back to square one.*

4. *Why does it have to be so difficult to lose weight?*

5. *We don't even want to talk about going on a diet.*

6. *Fear of being deprived or being constantly hungry, is a major stumbling block.*

The vicious cycle continues, and here we are still, needing to lose that weight! We can waste years of our lives on this struggle. We are also prone to end up even heavier than we were before we started a diet, every time one of those diets fails us. After a while, you begin to feel like a yo-yo, bouncing up and down. Where does it end?

Eventually, most of us just give up and decide that there is nothing we can do. This is the point at which obesity related medical conditions take hold. People who are overweight have a very high risk of developing Type 2 Diabetes, high cholesterol and serious heart conditions. To prevent these conditions all we have to do is lose weight and get healthier. Yea, right! We've already tried that and tried that and tried that again!

It's Easy to Lose Weight and Keep it Off!

Go ahead and chuck all of those preconceived notions about weight loss, along with all the latest fad diets right out the window!

In this book we have already learned some of the many benefits of adding Green Smoothies to your diet. They are easy to make, they are delicious, they are healthy and nutritious, they detox the body, ***and believe it or not, they will help you lose weight easily!***

Even one green smoothie a day, used as replacement for one meal or a snack, will put you on the road to permanent weight loss and better health. It will increase your metabolism, reawaken your taste buds, and kill those sugar cravings, while giving you a craving for even more healthy food. This will naturally and easily lead to eating healthier at every meal, because that will be what your body is telling you that it wants. Even if you lead a sedentary lifestyle or you work sitting at a desk all day, you will lose weight and feel better!

Yes, it is also true that exercise is a necessary part of any weight loss process or healthy lifestyle. The trick to green smoothies is that they give you lots of energy, naturally. It is impossible to resist getting up on your feet and doing something! You may have a sudden urge to learn a new sport, get out and play ball with your kids, or just take that long relaxing walk that you just haven't found the energy for. 30 minutes is sufficient when you are just starting to exercise. Although exercise is essential to optimum weight and health, you don't have to sweat the small stuff, let it take care of itself!

I am not telling you that your excess weight is going to magically disappear overnight. However, I guarantee that if you merely replace one meal a day with a healthy green smoothie, it will not be very long before you notice those clothes getting looser and looser. Just another incentive to give it a try; a shopping trip, and this time for smaller clothes!

How the Food You Eat Helps You Lose Weight

The body has certain nutritional requirements that must be met in order to achieve and maintain a healthy weight. While it would seem to be common sense that sugar and fat contribute to an overweight condition, it all depends on the type of sugar or fat, and the amount of them that you consume.

In Green Smoothies fruit is your base ingredient. Fruit does contain sugar, in the natural form of sucrose and glucose. Some fruits can also high in calories. It is also true, that the natural sugar found in fruit is vital to the body to fuel all of its processes. All of the cells in your body actually feed on these natural sugars. The body requires these calories and the carbohydrates in fruit, in order to create *energy*.

Energy is what it takes for the body to metabolize your food Refined and processed sugar, such as white cane sugar or the sugars found in processed foods are a very different thing. The body has absolutely no need for this type of sugar and it will cause weight gain. The fruits that you use as a base in smoothies are also packed with fiber which aids your digestion and detox routines, and contributes to weight loss.

The greens that make up the other part of your smoothie ingredients provide you with Vitamin K which is not found in many other foods, phytonutrients that are thought to help prevent many diseases and tons of additional fiber for digestive health. You are also getting substantial amounts of protein and calcium, which are the nutrients that you get from meat and dairy products. The problem with meat and dairy are the bad fats they contain. **If you want to lose weight, you should cut down your good fats to 20 or 25 % of the total calories you take in every day.**

While it is not recommended here to become a vegetarian or raw food junkie, it does help to reduce the amount of meat and dairy in your diet. When you do eat these foods, eat lean meat and low-fat or non-fat dairy products. Don't misunderstand and think that this means that you cannot eat any foods that you like just because you want to. You can. As long as you continue your daily green smoothies, feel free to treat yourself to almost anything once a week. One more time; to try to avoid packaged and processed foods containing chemicals and preservatives. These products only undermine all of your good green smoothie work. *The main thing to keep in mind is that enough is enough, and anything more than that is too much!*

Let's See if We Can Bust Some of those Old Weight Loss Myths!

1. *Just Count Calories* – Who hasn't tried this one? Counting calories and trying to reduce them as you go never works. When your weight loss expectations don't meet how few calories you are consuming, then the frustration sets in. It is more important

where the calories come from than how many there are. There does have to be a limit somewhere, but common sense is your indicator where that might be.

2. ***Carbohydrates are Fattening*** – Fruit is full of carbohydrates and they actually boost your weight loss! Just like calories, carbohydrates from fruits and vegetables are good. If they come from other less than healthy foods, then they are bad carbohydrates that can cause weight gain. Carbohydrates are the fuel that allows your body to burn fat and give you energy. Good carb foods are full of fiber and we all know we need all of that we can get. While some believe that all carbohydrates are the same, this is simply not true.

3. ***Fats are Bad*** – We have also explored the truth about fats. We learned that there are both good and bad fats. The good fats are necessary for the body to be healthy. They can make you gain weight, but only if you exceed the 20 to 25% of your calorie intake rule for fats.

4. ***If You Don't Eat, You Will Lose Weight*** – Although, it may be hard to understand how this is not true; it really isn't. Skipping a meal tells the body that it should begin to store more fat in order to stave off starvation. This is an inherent body mechanism against starvation, and you have no control over it if you do not eat.

5. ***Refuse Regular Weight Checks*** – This one is a personal choice. Other than waiting for your clothes to get too big, weighing yourself is how you know if you are making any progress in your weight loss quest. On the other hand, many people get discouraged by weighing themselves every day, and then being disappointed when they do not see as much weight loss as they think they should. Once a week weigh-ins should be sufficient, and will give you more to look forward to the next week. Weighing yourself can become an obsessive problem.

6. **Snacking is a NO-NO** – So wrong! Healthy snacks like green smoothies will help to control your hunger and reduce the danger of over-eating at meals. It also makes it easier to resist the things that really are bad for you.

7. **Do Not Eat Later than 8:00 pm** – Your body cannot tell time! The only reason that you need to limit your intake in the evening after dinner, is because it is normal to be less active at that time of day. If you just sit around in the evening, then your body is not using up any excess calories. This can interfere with your sleep as well.

Now we are learning some new and improved facts that can help to make losing weight an easier journey. We have also found out that some of the things we have always believed about weight loss are simply not true!

While fruits and vegetables in general are all good for weight loss, there are a few that really super power your weight loss Green Smoothies. Low calorie and high fiber are the keys to giving your weight loss a quick and effective starting point. Try adding some of these foods to your weight loss smoothie.

Grapefruit

Pumpkin (cooked has the best flavor)

Kale

Apples

Blueberries

Pomegranates

Chia Seeds

Raspberries

Pears

Strawberries

Bananas

Oranges

Broccoli

Celery

Cucumber

Carrots

Any and all leafy greens

Weight Loss Smoothie Recipes

Now that we know what we need to know about losing weight with green smoothies, it is time to get on with the enjoyable task of making some of those "oh so delicious treats" that will also help us find that slim and trim person within!

Pineapple Pear Berry Smoothie

This is a delicious way for berry lovers to get started with weight loss smoothies.

> 1 cup Pineapple, peeled, cored and cut up
> 2 cups each Strawberries and Blueberries, fresh or frozen
> 2 Pears, peeled, cored and chopped
> 1 tsp. Chia Seeds (optional)
> 3 cups Baby Spinach, chopped
> ½ cup Water or Crushed Ice

Place all ingredients except spinach in the blender and pulse to mix. Add spinach and blend on high until you achieve a creamy texture. Makes 1 Large Serving (meal replacement size)

Nutrition: 337 calories, 3 grams fat, 7 grams protein, 93 grams carbs, 21 grams fiber, calcium, iron Vitamins A and C.

Banana Razz-Ma-Tazz Smoothie

If you like the tartness of raspberry and the smooth creaminess of banana, you'll love this!
>1 Banana, frozen and peeled
>1 cup Raspberries, fresh or frozen
>2 tsp. Chia Seeds, soaked
>½ cup Water or Crushed Ice
>3 cups Baby Spinach

Blend all ingredients on high until creamy and smooth.
Makes 1 Serving

Nutrition: 213 calories, 6 grams protein, 47 grams carbs, 3 grams fat and 14.9 grams fiber.

Peachy Mango Dream Smoothie

A little tropical, a little green, and sooo good!
>2 Mangos, peeled, pitted and chopped
>1 Peach, peeled and pitted
>½ cup Water or Crushed Ice
>5 cups Baby Spinach

Blend all ingredients on high until smooth.
Makes 1 Serving

Nutrition: 235 calories, 6 grams protein, 57 grams carbs, 1 gram fat and 9.5 grams of fiber.

The following two recipes contain far more calories than the ones above. These are intended as meal replacement smoothies for weight loss. Don't let the amount of calories fool you; if you have one of these in place of breakfast or lunch, you will lose weight and still be full.

Plumberry Smoothie

Plums are the order of the day, plenty of sweet goodness here!
>   4 Plums, pitted
>   1 cup Blueberries, fresh or frozen
>   2 Bananas, frozen and peeled
>   ½ cup Water or Crushed Ice
>   1 head Romaine Lettuce

Blend all ingredients on high until smooth.
Makes 1 Serving

Nutrition: 478 calories, 12 grams protein, 28.2 grams fiber, calcium and iron.

Kale-n-Orange Weight Loss Smoothie

Who would have thought this combo could taste so sweet and refreshing!
>   2 Oranges, peeled and seeded
>   2 Bananas, frozen and peeled
>   ½ cup Water or Crushed Ice
>   3 cups Kale, chopped

Pulse all ingredients except kale until mixed well. Add kale and process on high until desire consistency is reached.
Makes 1 Serving

Nutrition: 447 calories, 12 grams protein, 16.3 grams fiber, calcium and iron.

In this chapter we have discovered the keys to successful weight loss using green smoothies.

1. How and why certain foods are effective at promoting weight loss.

2. How the body processes food and what foods it requires to be healthy and slim.

3. We've busted some old weight loss myths.

4. We discovered some more fabulous smoothie recipes.

In Chapter 5 we'll find out how to de-stress our lives with more excellent Green Smoothie recipes.

Beat
The Negative Effects Of
Stress

Stress can quite literally kill you. It makes you more likely to become ill; chronic stress is known to be a contributor to many chronic health problems. It is hard on your nerves, your heart and your digestion among other things.

When you are stressed out you find it impossible to enjoy anything. Of course a certain amount of stress is normal and your body and mind can handle it well. Long term stress that involves frustration, anger, job dissatisfaction, money problems, unhappy relationships and any one of a million other things that remain unresolved, can absolutely destroy your health both physically and mentally.

There is no denying that one of the side effects of stress is weight gain. Too much stress can lead to depression. For many of us, one of the major *"feel sorry for ourselves"* things that we do is eat. When you are stressed, especially at the end of a long day, what is your first thought? For most of us, it is *"I can't wait to get home, sit down and try to relax!"* However, the stress itself usually prevents the relaxation part of the equation from happening. What do we do instead? *"Have a snack; why not?" Do we get up then and go for a walk or do anything else? No. Did that snack make us feel better? No.* So, 9 times out of 10, we will either move right on to have an unhealthy dinner, have some more snacks, or pop on the tube and just sit there; maybe even all 3!

Just like anything else, stress cannot be removed from your life instantaneously, but there are things that you can do that will help.

1. Figure out exactly what is causing your stress. You are the only one who knows what the cause is, and the only one that can do anything about it.

2. Try meditation for about 10 minutes. Read a book about it or take a class.

3. Spend time outdoors, get a little sun, take a nature walk; even 15 minutes can refresh and rejuvenate you.

4. Look for a new job if that is the cause. Just stop with the unhappy relationship or any other social activity that is no longer satisfying and fulfilling for you.

5. Take time for yourself and read a book, listen to your favorite music, pamper yourself and take a soak in the tub. Anything that gets you away from the electronic jungle can be very relaxing.

6. *Add Green Smoothies to your diet, they really have the power to provide the healthy nutrients that your body needs to cope with stress and clear your mind!*

THIS IS A GREAT TIME TO HAVE A GREEN SMOOTHIE!

The Green Smoothie gives you that mega dose of natural and wholesome food just chock full of those nutrients you need. They energize you, and can help to improve your mood. Green Smoothies balance your hormones and help your body be prepared for, and deal with, stress. *When your body feels better, so will your mind.*

De-stressing Green Smoothie Recipes

De-Stress Me Green Smoothie

The pomegranate gives this one an extra flavor kick that can't be beat!

    1 Banana, frozen and peeled
    1 cup Blueberries, frozen
    ½ cup Red Grapes
    ½ cup Pomegranate Juice, fresh
    3 cups Baby Spinach, chopped

Mix all ingredients in blender except the spinach. Pulse a few times. Add the spinach and process on high until mixture is creamy.
Makes 1 Serving

Nutrition: 325 calories, 1 gram fat, 6 grams protein, 82 grams carbs, 12.6 grams fiber, calcium, iron, Vitamins A and C.

Green & Fruity De-Stress Smoothie

An amazingly tasty smoothie that is full of disease fighting ingredients.
> ½ Pink Grapefruit, peeled and seeded
> 1 Banana, frozen and peeled
> 1 Kiwi, chilled and peeled
> 2 cups each Kale and Baby Spinach, chopped
> 8 ounces Coconut Water, unsweetened

Pulse all ingredients in blender except greens until mixed. Add greens and blend on high until smooth.
Makes 1 Serving

Nutrition: 379 calories, 7 grams fat, 12 grams protein, 74 grams carbs, 13.1 grams fiber, calcium, Vitamins A, C, B1, B6 and K, folate, magnesium and potassium.

Stress Busting Green Smoothie

Easy, fruity and sweet, what could be better?
> 2 cups Water or Crushed Ice
> 2 Bananas, frozen and peeled
> 1 Apple, peeled, cored and chopped
> 1 Pear, peeled, cored and chopped
> 2 handfuls Baby Spinach, chopped

Place the water and fruit in the blender and pulse on high a few times. Switch to puree to blend thoroughly. Add the chopped greens and liquefy on high until the mixture is smooth and green and you cannot see any pieces of the greens. Pour in a glass and enjoy!
Makes 1 Serving

Nutrition: This one is low calorie, low cholesterol, fat free and contains potassium, antioxidants and iron.

Melon Head Green Smoothie

Relax and refresh with this light and delicious blend of greens and melons.

 1 cup Watermelon, fresh or frozen, seeded and cubed
 ½ cup Honey Dew Melon, seeded and cubed
 ½ cup Cantaloupe, seeded and cubed
 2 cups Kale, chopped

Pulse melons in blender about 3 times, add the Kale and process on high until smooth.
Makes 1 Serving

Nutrition: low calorie, super hydrating, has iron, protein, Vitamins C, A and K and fiber

Calming Tropical Mint Smoothie

Mint is calming yet refreshing at the same time, so sit back and relax with this one!

 2 cups Pineapple, peeled, cored and chopped
 1 Mango, peeled, pitted and chopped
 1 Banana, frozen and peeled
 1 cup each Dandelion Greens and Baby Spinach
 ½ bunch Mint, fresh

Combine all ingredients except greens and mint in blender and pulse a few times. Add greens and mint and blend on high until smooth and creamy. Garnish with additional mint if desired.
Makes 1 Serving

Nutrition: Vitamins A, C, K, potassium, iron, calcium, fiber, protein and antioxidants

In this chapter we have learned how stress affects our bodies and minds, and we have discovered some stress relieving methods to try. We also found some more great Green Smoothie recipes to add to our recipe books.

In Chapter 6 we will find out how to restore the energy we once had, and get it into our daily routines.

Boost Your Energy The Green Smoothie Way

Believe it or not, a Green Smoothie can give you all the energy your need to get your day off to the right start, help you get into your workout routine, or just anytime you need a little lift!

Unhealthy food is what zaps all of your energy in the first place, especially foods that are processed or have a lot of fat. The body uses up all of your energy trying to digest these foods, and that doesn't leave any energy for you to do anything else.

That is why whole food choices that are low in fat and sugar, and high in carbohydrates, are the foods that we use in Green Smoothies. Other factors contribute to a lack of energy as well: not enough sleep, not exercising and too much stress. Green Smoothies also tackle these problems, and that gives you a great all-around solution to all of these issues.

Having that Green Smoothie in the morning gives you a healthy alternative to the caffeine in coffee and energy drinks, that so many people depend on today to get their day started. When your nutrition is better, you sleep more restfully and naturally feel more energetic.

There is no need to do without the energy that you need every day. One of the easiest ways I know to get on track first thing in the morning is to have a Green Smoothie for breakfast. Just forget all of your preconceived notions of a healthy breakfast, and you will feel more energetic from the very first day that you replace that breakfast with a Green Smoothie.

What do you get in a Green Smoothie breakfast to boost your energy level?

1. Super Energy from Carbohydrates

2. Vitamins

3. Minerals

4. Antioxidants

5. Extra Hydration

6. You get full and stay full until lunchtime

Green Smoothies are also the best companion for an exercise routine. You need energy to exercise, and when you exercise you, lose weight, reduce stress, elevate your mood and improve your mental agility. You don't have to be a weight lifter or a runner, but it is important to strengthen your body. 20 to 30 minutes a day is all it takes: go for a long power walk, dance, swim, or go to an aerobics class or the gym. Whatever you can fit into your schedule will help. These Green Smoothie recipes will help you find the energy you need to get up and get moving. If you are going to have a smoothie before your exercise, give it about an hour to digest before you begin.

Energizing Green Smoothie Recipes

Green PowerShake Smoothie

This one is fruity, sweet and invigorating first thing in the morning.

    2 Bananas, frozen and peeled
    6 Strawberries, fresh or frozen
    ½ cup Red Grapes
    3 cups Baby Spinach or Mixed Greens, chopped
    ½ cup Water or Crushed Ice

Mix all ingredients except spinach in the blender and pulse a few times. Add the spinach and blend on high until creamy.
Makes 1 Serving

Nutrition: 367 calories, 2 grams fat, 8 grams protein, 89 grams carbs, 12.5 grams fiber, calcium, iron, Vitamins A and C.

Perfect Pre-Workout Green Smoothie

This delicious pear and orange combo takes the slightly bitter taste of kale and makes it disappear!

     2 Oranges, peeled and seeded
     1 Pear, peeled and cored
     2 cups Kale, chopped
     1 tsp. Chia Seeds, soaked
     ½ cup Water or Crushed Ice

Add all ingredients together in blender except the kale. Pulse several times to mix. Add the kale and blend on high until creamy.
Makes 1 Serving

Nutrition: 358 calories, 3 grams fat, 9 grams protein, 86 grams carbs, 17.5 grams fiber, calcium, iron, Vitamins A and C.

Post Workout Green Smoothie

Replenish your nutrients and hydrate after your workout with this classic peach/mango combo.

     1 Mango, peeled and pitted
     1 Peach, peeled and pitted
     1 head Romaine Lettuce, chopped
     ½ cup Water or Crushed Ice
     2 tbsp. Chia Seeds, soaked

Mix all ingredients in blender except lettuce. Pulse several times, add the lettuce and blend on high until smooth.
Makes 1 Serving

Nutrition: 375 calories, 4 grams fat, 10 grams protein, 83 grams carbs, 16.4 grams fiber, calcium, iron, Vitamins A and C.

Super Charger Green Smoothie

This one has tons of energy foods to give you that extra boost anytime you need it!

    1 Banana, frozen and peeled

    1 Orange, peeled and seeded

    ½ cup Coconut, shredded

    ½ cup Goji Berries and 2 tbsp. Chia Seeds, soaked together for 10 minutes

    2 cups Parsley and 1 cup Kale, chopped

    Spearmint Leaves, fresh and Cinnamon to taste

Combine ingredients except for greens and spearmint in blender and pulse. Add greens and spearmint leaves and process on high until smooth. Add water if needed to thin mixture.

Makes 1 Serving

Nutrition: Vitamins C, A, K and B vitamins, potassium, calcium, iron, protein, fiber, antioxidants, Omega 3 Fatty Acids

Up & Up Green Smoothie

This one is packed with energy delivering nutrients, and it tastes great!

    1 Orange, peeled and seeded

    1 Mango, peeled and pitted

    ½ cup Goji Berries, soaked for 10 minutes

    ½ cup Water or Crushed Ice

    2 cups Parsley, chopped

Mix all ingredients in blender except parsley. Pulse several times and then add parsley. Process on high until the mixture is smooth and creamy.

Makes 1 Serving

Nutrition: antioxidants, Vitamin C, A and K, iron, protein, fiber

In this chapter we have discovered how Green Smoothies provide us with the extra energy needed to boost our weight loss and exercise goals. We also found a few more fabulous smoothie recipes to try.

In Chapter 7 we will find out how Green Smoothies help with mental clarity and mood enhancement.

Improve Your Mood
And Mental Agility

If you want to improve your moods, and mental agility and clarity, then Green Smoothies are just the ticket. The brain is an organ, just like all the others in your body and it requires high levels of healthy nutrients to be happy and healthy. If the brain is not happy and healthy, then you are not. It is not only with stress that your hormones play an important role. Balanced hormones have a lot to do with your mood, and especially your *happiness quotient!*

Many people notice the difference in the way that they feel the very first time they have a big Green Smoothie! However, the mood elevation and higher spirits will increase as you go along with a daily Green Smoothie or two. They can help to alleviate depression, assist with remaining calm in stressful situations and allow you to relax more. Besides, you are naturally going to feel much better when you are energized, and that is another thing that Green Smoothies do for you.

Many Green Smoothie users have reported that they no longer need medication for depression and anxiety since they began having their daily dose of green Smoothie. *However, never stop taking any medication without consulting your physician!* They report a new ability to remain calm and focused, as well as clarity of thought that is not possible with chemical medications.

When we eat all those processed foods that we are used to every day, the ingredients and sugar have a negative effect on the brain, as well as the body. The Green Smoothie will clear all those toxins out and you will face the world with a clear mind and a new feeling of creativity.

Try some of these great Green Smoothie Recipes and see how much better you feel!

Mood Enhancing Green Smoothie Recipes

Refreshing Purple Smoothie

This smoothie is a delicious and energizing full meal deal! Great as a replacement for breakfast or lunch!

> 1 Banana, frozen and peeled
> 1 cup Blueberries, frozen
> 2 Peaches, peeled and pitted
> ½ Beet, fresh, raw, peeled
> 1 Carrot, chopped
> 1 bunch Bok Choy, chopped
> ½ cup Water or Crushed Ice

Mix all ingredients in blender except Bok Choy and pulse several times. Add Bok Choy and blend on high until purple and creamy.
Makes 1 Large Serving

Nutrition: 406 calories, 1 gram fat, 8 grams protein, 96 grams carbs, 19 grams fiber, calcium, iron, Vitamins A, C, B1 – B6 and K, copper, magnesium, manganese, phosphorus, potassium, lutein ,lycopene and phytonutrients.

Green Bananas Smoothie

Satisfying and delicious, this one is great to relax with at the end of the day. You'll soon find your mood soaring!

    2 Bananas, frozen and peeled
    1 Nectarine, peeled and pitted
    4 Strawberries, fresh or frozen
    3 Dates, pitted and chopped
    2 to 3 cups Greens (your choice)
    ½ cup Water or Crushed Ice

Pulse all ingredients except greens a few times. Add greens and blend on high until smooth. Add additional water if mixture is too thick.

Nutrition: low fat, Vitamins, A, C, K, iron, potassium, protein, fiber, antioxidants

Figgy Pear Green Smoothie

The flavor and sweetness of the fig and pear combo tames the taste of the kale and makes a delicious treat!

    1 Pear, peeled, cored and chopped
    4 Figs, chopped
    1 cup Kale, chopped
    ½ cup Water or Crushed Ice

Blend all ingredients except kale until well mixed. Add kale and blend on high 30 seconds.

Nutrition: Vitamin C and K, iron, fiber and antioxidants

P & P Green Smoothie

Pineapple and Papaya are and irresistible taste combination!
>1 Papaya, peeled and seeded
>1 cup Pineapple, peeled and cored
>2 to 3 cups Kale or Baby Spinach
>½ cup Water or Crushed Ice

Pulse 3 times in blender all ingredients except greens. Add the greens and process on high until smooth.

>**Hint: Add ½ tsp. Coconut extract for an even more tropical taste treat.**

Nutrition: low calorie, low fat, packed with Vitamins, minerals and antioxidants

Apple Berry Green Smoothie

Sweet berries and apple make this one more like a dessert than a nutritious food!
>1 Apple, sweet variety, peeled, cored and chopped
>1 cup Mixed Berries, frozen (your choice)
>½ cup Water or Crushed Ice
>2 cups Baby Spinach, chopped (or other greens of your choice)

Pulse all ingredients except spinach in blender. Add the spinach and blend on high until smooth.
Makes 1 Serving

Nutrition: low fat, with iron, fiber, antioxidants, Vitamin C

In this chapter we have discovered how Green Smoothies can improve your mood and enhance your brain function, and we found even more delicious Green Smoothie recipes!

In Chapter 8 we will discuss how Green Smoothies can boost your immune system and help you sail through cold and flu season, as well as help to prevent other diseases.

Boost Your Immune System

We all know that Vitamin C is the most commonly known nutrient to boost the immune system. Many people drink a lot of orange juice or take supplemental Vitamin C especially during cold and flu season. *What has not been recognized is that you can get mega doses of Vitamin C from your favorite Green Smoothie!* Not only do citrus fruits and strawberries contain massive amounts of Vitamin C, but *so do the greens you use in your smoothie!*

Boosting your immune system is not only about fighting colds and flu. The immune system is what fights all infections, viruses and bacteria that enter the body. It is also the main line of defense that you have to resist serious diseases such as diabetes, heart conditions and cancer.

Here are some of the best ingredients you can use to make *Super Immune Boosting Green Smoothies!*

Greens of all kinds are filled with protein, iron, phytonutrients, antioxidants, minerals and Vitamins including K and C, which is your best infection fighting vitamin.

Strawberries have more Vitamin C than citrus fruit plus zinc, Vitamins A and B6, antioxidants and flavonoids.

Citrus Fruits full of Vitamin C can help prevent respiratory infections and heal sore throats.

Blueberries have concentrated antioxidants, antibacterial and antibiotic properties.

Honey has anti-inflammatory, antibacterial and antibiotic properties, as well as antioxidants. If you need a little natural sweetness for your smoothie, get it here.

Green Tea contains concentrated amounts of antioxidants.

Cantaloupe is rich in Vitamin A and C. These powerful antioxidant vitamins promote healthy skin, and after all, your skin is by far the largest organ of the body, and it is the barrier between you and infection and environmental pollutants.

Carrots are another food that is very high in Vitamin A and low calorie, as well. Vitamin A is vital to eye health, skin health and immune system health.

Blackberries are full of zinc which is very important to strengthen a weak immune system. Zinc helps to build our infection fighting cells, and foods rich in this mineral are perfect when you are fighting cancer or any other disease that depletes the immune system.

Goji Berries are relatively new on the market. They come from Tibet and are full of antioxidants and give you extra energy. They can be found at grocery stores, health food stores or online.

Bananas are rich in potassium, which is easily depleted from the body if you have high blood pressure, infections or other illnesses.

Mangos are rich in Vitamin A as beta carotene and antioxidants, fiber and Vitamin C.

Papaya is chock full of good immune boosting nutrients: Vitamins A, C, B1, B2, B3, B6, B9, calcium, iron, fiber, protein, iron and calcium

Chia or Flax Seeds provide extra protein and antioxidants, along with essential Omega 3 Fatty Acids.

Immune Boosting Green Smoothie Recipes

Green Banana Berry Smoothie

This is sweet and provides super immune boosting nutrition!

    1 Banana, frozen and peeled
    5 Strawberries, fresh or frozen
    2 cups Baby Spinach or other Greens, chopped
    2 tsp. Honey (or to taste)
    ½ cup Green Tea or Green Tea Ice Cubes crushed

Place all ingredients except greens into the blender a pulse a few times. Add the greens and blend until smooth.
Makes 1 Serving

> *Hint: Add a tablespoon of Chia Seeds and ½ cup Goji Berries soaked together for 10 minutes for an even bigger serving of nutrients.*

Nutrition: low calorie, low fat, Vitamins K and C, iron, calcium, protein, fiber, antioxidants and Omega 3s

Green and Citrusy Immune Booster

This one is a little tart, a little sweet, and the vanilla makes it scrumptious!

    1 Orange, peeled and seeded
    ½ Pink Grapefruit, peeled and seeded
    1 cup Cantaloupe, peeled and seeded
    2 tsp. or more Honey
    2 cups Greens, chopped
    ½ tsp. Pure Vanilla Extract

Pulse all ingredients except the greens in the blender a few times. Add greens and process on high until smooth.
Makes 1 Serving

> **Hint: Add a little grated Ginger for an extra kick. Ginger adds carbs, fiber, protein, Vitamin C, phosphorus and potassium.**

Nutrition: basic recipe is low calorie, low fat, has Vitamins A, C and B, iron, potassium, calcium, protein, and has antioxidants, anti-inflammatories and antibiotic properties.

Mango Berry Bonanza Smoothie

A hint of berry and citrus and this one smells as good as it tastes!

    1 Mango, peeled and pitted
    ½ cup each Blackberries, fresh and Blueberries, frozen
    1 Orange, peeled and seeded
    1 tsp. Honey
    3 cups Greens (your choice)

Place all ingredients except greens in blender and pulse. Add greens and blend on high until smooth.
Makes 1 Serving

Nutrition; Plenty of Vitamin C and A, antioxidants, iron, zinc, calcium, protein, anti-inflammatories, antivirals and antibiotics, low in calories and fat

Papamango Immune Booster

Tropical fruit and greens, how much better does it get?

  ½ each Papaya and Mango, peeled and seeded
  1 Banana, frozen and peeled
  1 Orange, peeled and seeded
  3 cups Greens, chopped
  ½ cup crushed Green Tea Ice

Mix all ingredients except greens in blender and pulse a few times. Add greens and process on high until super creamy.
Makes 1 Serving

Nutrition: low calorie, Vitamins A& C, iron, calcium, fiber, antioxidants, potassium

Bananaloupe Green Smoothie

Super nutritious and just as delicious; a sweet creamy smoothie you will love!

  1 Carrot, chopped or grated
  1 cup Cantaloupe, peeled, seeded and chopped
  1 Banana, frozen and peeled
  3 cups Greens (your choice) chopped
  ½ cup Green Tea or crushed Green Tea Ice Cubes

Except for greens pulse remaining ingredients in blender several times, then add greens and blend on high until thick and smooth.

Nutrition: Antioxidants, Vitamins C, A and K, iron, potassium, protein and calcium

In this chapter we have learned what out immune system needs to be healthy and effective and how to help it along its way. We found some more smoothie recipes to try as well.

In Chapter 9 we will talk about the benefits that Green Smoothies have for your hair and skin.

Strong, Healthy Hair & Beatiful Nails

Believe it or not, the health of your skin and hair has less to do with what you put on it, than what you put in your body to nourish it!

You can spend a fortune these days on skin products that claim to reduce wrinkles, to cure dry skin, to erase age spots, to cure acne, and any number of skin problems. The same can be said for hair products; they promise silky smooth hair (even if you weren't born with it), they will help your hair to grow, or they will cure scalp disorders. The truth is that whatever type of skin and hair you were born with is the type that you have. You cannot inherently change that.

What you can do is make sure that your skin and hair are always at their absolute best by giving them proper nutrition. *Green Smoothies contain every nutrient, in abundance that is required by skin and hair to be healthy and youthful far longer than any other so called cure!*

Don't get me wrong, I use hand lotion, shampoo and conditioner. These things have their place in your personal hygiene routine, and for temporary relief of such things as dry skin. However, if you use ingredients in your Green Smoothies that address the problems associated with skin and hair, you will be amazed at the difference it will make. *Just leave the potions and supplements and treatments, and fall back on nutrition; it is the only thing guaranteed to improve the condition of hair and skin!*

Let's Start with Your Hair

The first thing that we need to understand about our hair is that *the ¼ to ½ inch of new hair growth that you see every month is dead; just as dead as dead can be!*

Whatever condition it was it when it grew out of your scalp is how it will be. The key is to give proper nutrition to the formation of the hair in the follicle so that it comes out healthy and looking its best. If you have thin hair, then you have to live with thin hair and the same can be said for thick hair, curly hair or wiry hair.

"Hair is a barometer of your overall health."
(David H. Kingsley, Ph.D., British Science Corporation, New York City, hair and scalp expert)

Your body does not recognize your hair to be essential to anything, simply because it is serves no useful purpose to the body's processes. If you go on fad diets or starve yourself, the body will remove the nutrients essential to healthy hair and employ them elsewhere for use by organs such as the brain or heart. This is referred to as starvation mode, and yet one more reason that such diets do not work and are not good for you. You can usually tell a long term dieter by the appearance of their hair.

Another thing that we have already learned is that Green Smoothie nutrition can balance your hormones. Hormones not only have an effect on mood, weight loss and all of those other issues; skin and hair are no different.

So how do you lose weight, stay healthy and still have great hair?

Green Smoothies made with a variety of ingredients that contain the essential nutrients that healthy hair production requires, will basically be the same ones that you use for good general health. Here are the essential nutrients needed for healthy hair production and in what smoothie ingredients you can find them.

Omega 3 Fatty Acids condition the hair and support the health of your scalp – flax seeds, walnuts

Zinc is a powerful antioxidant and deficiencies can cause hair loss – legumes such as kidney beans and lentils, walnuts, cashews, pecans, almonds

Protein promotes the growth of hair; it is what hair is made of. – legumes, leafy greens, avocado, nuts and seeds

Biotin deficiency causes brittle hair and it assists in hair production – legumes, bananas, spinach, avocado

Iron stimulates the replenishment of hair – leafy greens, legumes

Calcium – leafy greens and many fruits

Vitamin A or Beta Carotene is vital to the production of sebum, the body's own hair conditioner – spinach, broccoli, Swiss chard, carrots

Vitamin C helps with sebum – spinach, broccoli, Swiss chard

Selenium is important in scalp health – Brazil nuts

Vitamins B6 and B12 strengthens the cuticle or outer surface of the hair and are vital to hair production in the follicle – bananas, spinach, blackberries, cantaloupe, walnuts, sunflower seeds, grapefruit, lime, wheat germ

Vitamin E increases blood circulation in the scalp which helps hair to grow. – spinach, wheat germ, asparagus, avocados, almonds

Of course, this is only a partial list of the foods in which you find these nutrients; additional options can be found in Green Smoothie recipes and ingredients in previous chapters.

What you need to know about nutrition for the skin?

The first and most important thing that we need to keep in mind about the skin is that it is the largest organ (and yes, it is an organ) of the body. It is also our defensive line against environmental contaminants, infections and other contagious diseases. That makes the nutrition of the skin a vitally important part of our health and nutrition regimen.

Because the skin is on the outside and bears the brunt of every unhealthy thing it comes in contact with, it tends to damage more easily and age more swiftly that our internal organs. However, all is not lost; Green Smoothies have the power to help your skin stay younger and healthier longer. You will find that the same nutrients that feed the inside and the hair also feed the skin.

So, exactly what does the skin need?

The skin needs hydration; there is no such thing as too much water, ever! The skin needs the nutrients that are found in the vegetables and fruits that we use to make Green Smoothies; no kidding!

According to experts, a wide variety of different vegetables and fruits of different colors should be on your list, because different colors of food contain different nutrients.

The main skin nutrients that promote cell replenishment and help to prevent wrinkles and sun damage are:

Antioxidants which control damage done to the skin by free radicals. This includes wrinkles. These nutrients include Vitamins A, C, E, Zinc, Lycopene (tomatoes), d-limonene (citrus), Selenium

Omega 3 Fatty Acids keep the skin strong and elastic to help keep out toxins.

Water essential to the whole body's moisture content and skin needs just as much since it is exposed to the air. Improper hydration leads to dry, flaky skin and more pronounced wrinkling.

Protein

Calcium

What are some of the best "skin foods?"

Watermelon is a red food that has high levels of beta carotene (Vitamin A) and lycopene. These antioxidants help protect you from damaging UV rays. Since these nutrients are held in the outer layer of the skin, they can also help to repair sun damage.

Almonds, Pumpkin Seeds and Sunflower Seeds are excellent sources of Vitamin E. E helps protect from free radicals that damage skin and improves both the texture and the quality.

Cucumber Peel is actually silica which is the major building block of collagen which plumps cells and prevents wrinkles. You will need home-grown or organic cucumbers as commercial ones have wax on the peeling. Of course, the cucumber as a whole is a good source of Vitamin C as well.

Citrus Zest or the grated peel of citrus fruits is known to reduce the risk of getting skin cancer about 30%. The active ingredient is d-limonene. Of course, citrus fruit itself is loaded with Vitamin C, another powerful antioxidant.

Broccoli contains sulforaphane which helps enzymes in the cells to work at their full protective capacity. This substance helps protect against UV rays.

Pomegranate is rich with antioxidants that help create collagen and promote healing.

Green Tea is another antioxidant rich plant which we have already explored using in place of water in our smoothie recipes.

Avocados are loaded with Omega 3 fatty acids, Vitamin E and biotin, which help prevent or reduce dry skin.

Tomatoes are rich in lycopene and beta carotene. They can help reduce the risk of sunburn and free radical damage.

There are many more vegetables and fruits that offer these beneficial nutrients, and we have already made many Green Smoothies that contain these ingredients. That means we already have a head start on improving our skin!

Do you notice a pattern here? These are the same nutrients from the same sources that we have been talking about in every chapter.

Hint: Avoiding Alcohol, Caffeine and Smoking can help to slow the dehydrations of skin and the onset of wrinkles.

Green Smoothie Recipes for Hair and Skin Health

Radiant Skin Smoothie

This one has a tasty tropical flavor everyone will love!

    1 Banana, frozen and peeled
    1 ½ cups Mango, peeled, seeded, cubed, frozen
    1 1/2 cups Coconut Water, fresh or frozen and crushed
    2 cups Mixed Spring Greens, chopped
    Sprig of Basil (optional)

Combine ingredients except greens and basil in blender and pulse several times. Add greens and basil and blend on high until smooth and creamy.

Makes 1 Serving

Nutrition: low calorie and loaded with antioxidants, minerals and vitamins.

Whole New You Green Smoothie

This one is veggie and fruity, with all the good stuff for healthy glowing skin!

      1 Banana, frozen and peeled
      1 each Apple & Pear, peeled, cored and chopped
      2 cups each Romaine Lettuce & Baby Spinach, chopped
      2 stalks Celery, chopped
      2 tbsp. Lemon Juice, fresh

Place all ingredients except greens in the blender and pulse several times. Add the greens and blend on high until smooth and creamy.
Makes 2 Servings

> **Hint:** *Adding a little Cilantro, Parsley or Cucumber ups the nutrition and the taste.*

Nutrition: *low calorie, chock full of antioxidants, B Vitamins, fiber and protein*

Fresh Face Green Smoothie

This one is very veggie with a tropical twist that is accented by the flavor of ginger.

      2 cups Pineapple, peeled, cored, chopped
      1 Orange, peeled and seeded
      4 stalks Celery, chopped
      1 Cucumber, chopped
      2 cups each Kale and Cilantro, chopped
      2 cups Coconut Water, frozen and crushed
      Ginger to taste

Place all ingredients except greens in blender and pulse several times.
Add greens and process until smooth.
Makes 2 Servings

Hint: *If you want some of those great Omega 3s in there, throw in some flax seed or wheat germ.*

Nutrition: low in fat, high in antioxidants, B Vitamins, iron, protein, calcium

---

Berry Good Complexion Smoothie

This one is berry sweet with extra antioxidants from Green Tea.
> 1 Banana, frozen and peeled
> 1 ½ cups Mixed Berries, frozen
> 3 cups Greens (your choice or mixed)
> ½ cup Green Tea, frozen and crushed

Place ingredients other than greens in blender and pulse a few times. Add greens and blend until smooth.
Makes 1 Serving

Nutrition: low calorie with antioxidants galore, potassium, protein, iron and B Vitamins

---

Acne Busting Green Smoothie

This one tastes good and will help to fight acne!
> 1 Orange, peeled and seeded
> 1 Kiwi, peeled
> 2 cups Baby Spinach
> 1 tbsp. Apple Cider Vinegar
> 2 tbsp. Honey (or to taste)
> Ginger, ground (optional)

Place ingredients except spinach in blender and pulse 2 to 3 times. Add spinach and blend on high about 30 seconds or until desires consistency.
Makes 1 Serving

Nutrition: low calorie, antioxidant rich, enzymes, iron, B Vitamins, protein

---

Hint: Honey and Apple Cider Vinegar are a great combination for fighting or preventing outbreaks of acne. Honey is anti-inflammatory, antiseptic and antibiotic; Apple Cider Vinegar (it needs to be unprocessed, unpasteurized and all-natural) contains enzymes that fight infections such as acne and yeast. If you add a tablespoon to anything containing berries or citrus fruits, you cannot taste it. It is also said to aid in weight loss.

In this chapter we learned how Green Smoothie ingredients are vital to hair and skin nutrition, so that we can stay younger looking as long as possible. We got to try out some interesting new smoothie recipes and we discovered that Green Smoothies in general take care of all facets of our health and weight.

In Chapter 10 we will learn a few more tips for customizing our smoothies to suit our taste without losing the nutritional value, and maybe even boosting it a bit more!

Customizing Your Green Smoothies

You can find inspiration in amazing and unusual places!

Ideas for your own custom smoothies can come from the most unusual places sometimes. You could be strolling down the grocery aisle and see an interesting new fruit, or a colorful vegetable that you hadn't thought of using in your smoothies before. Maybe you notice a box of kid's fruit snacks, and something about the fruit combinations they use catches your eye. Perhaps you walk into a shop and smell a delightfully different candle that reminds you of a favorite spice you haven't tried using in smoothies yet. ***You just never know where you might find inspiration for your smoothie experiments!***

One of the first stops anyone making smoothies should make is the spice rack. Chances are good that the spices you like in vegetable dishes and desserts will be equally as good in a smoothie. Many spices have great nutritional benefits and natural healing abilities. ***That sounds like a perfect combination!***

There are many options for finding tasty ways to boost the nutrients and tastiness of green smoothies. ***Super Foods*** are all the rage today. Many of them are quite flavorful, and enhance the taste and nutrition of foods to which they are added. The most popular ones are now available at your grocers in the organic or health food aisles. Others might only be found in a health food store or online. Here are a few for your consideration.

Flax Seed–Flax seeds have fiber, protein, Omega 3 fatty acids, Vitamins B1, B2, B3, B5, B6, B9 and C. It also provides calcium, iron, magnesium, phosphorus, potassium and zinc. (Flax seeds should be ground with a coffee grinder before adding them to smoothies.)

Wheat Germ – Wheat germ gives a concentrated dose of several nutrients, such as Folic acid, zinc, magnesium, Omega 3 Fatty Acids, Vitamin E and thiamine, as well as lots of fiber.

Chia Seeds – This little seeds form a paste when soaked in water. They make an excellent thickening agent for any type of food or smoothie. They also contain such nutrients as fiber, phosphorus, manganese, potassium, iron, molybdenum, zinc, copper, niacin, Omega 3 Fatty Acids and antioxidants. They are low in fat and cholesterol free. Chia Seeds are a South American product that does not grow in the U.S. Therefore, the best way to obtain them is ordering online.

Goji Berries – These berries come from China. They are fairly common in health food stores. They contain amino acids, essential fatty acids, beta-carotene, lutein, lycopene, antioxidants, calcium, potassium, iron, zinc, selenium, riboflavin and Vitamin C. *That is pretty potent berry!*

Alfalfa Sprouts – These can be found at your local grocery store. They have a light flavor that is very good on food or salads. They are equally good as an additive to Green Smoothies. They contain a lot of protein and calcium, plus B Vitamins, Vitamins C, D and E. They have medicinal value and can help improve digestion and relieve some kidney disorders.

Garlic – If you try a totally veggie and greens smoothie, Garlic might be just the ticket. It is good for your immune system, reduces cholesterol, helps prevent cancer, and has been shown to help those with heart disease. It has fiber, protein, beta-carotene, thiamine, riboflavin, niacin, Vitamins B5, B6, B9 and C. It also has calcium, iron, magnesium, phosphorus, potassium, zinc, manganese and selenium. ***Talk about antioxidants!***

These are only a very few of the excellent all-natural additives, or ***"Super Foods"*** that you can use in your Green Smoothies. Many of them are far more exotic, hard to find and expensive than the ones above.

10 Tips for Getting the Most out of Your Green Smoothie

1. The fruits that you choose for your smoothies should always be ripe. Unripe or semi-ripe fruit will not sufficiently sweeten your smoothie and can give it a bitter tang.

2. Water that you use in smoothies should always be bottled or purified.

3. Thicken a smoothie by adding crushed ice or thin it by adding water.

4. Don't refuse to try new greens in your smoothies just because you think you won't like it. Make a small portion, add spices, flavorings or honey until you get it just right.

5. As you may have noticed some of the recipes in this book call for mixed greens or more than one green. This is a great way to get all the benefits of the greens, without having to taste just a single one.

6. Don't refuse to try new fruits that you don't like to eat plain. You may find that in combination with other fruits and vegetables that they add that special "oomph" that your recipe needed.

7. Nuts have tons of protein, minerals and Omega 3s that your body needs. Many even have antioxidant properties. You can grind them and add them to your Green Smoothies. You can also soak them and use the water (referred to as nut milk) in

place of the water in your smoothies; all the taste and nutrition without the grit. Try garnishing your smoothie with nuts, or just have a handful with your smoothie.

8. Seeds are another great addition, and there are many to choose from other than those listed above. Sunflower seeds, Pumpkin seeds, Celery seeds and a host of others offer extra nutrition and added taste choices.

9. Try having an all-veggie smoothie for an interesting alternative. You can add salt, pepper, garlic, hot spices or anything you desire to make it taste just right.

10. The most important tip of all is experiment, experiment and then experiment some more. The more you do, the better your Green Smoothies will taste, and soon you will be telling everyone else how to make them and what they can do for you.

Here is a bonus recipe for you to try. I love this one. It is an all-veggie Green Smoothie (except for a little lime) that reminds me of one of my favorite alcoholic beverages. I call it

My Bloody Mary Green Smoothie

The veggies and spices make this taste very much like a virgin Bloody Mary!

2 Red Tomatoes, chopped
6 leaves Red Leaf Lettuce, chopped
¼ bunch Basil, fresh
2 sticks Celery, chopped
½ Red Onion, peeled and chopped
¼ Avocado, peeled and pitted
½ Lime, juiced
1 clove Garlic, peeled and chopped
1 cup Crushed Ice (or more if needed)
Sea Salt, Black Pepper, Cayenne Pepper to taste

Mix all ingredients except lettuce and basil in blender and pulse several times. Add greens and blend on high until desired consistency. (More ice or water may be added to thicken or thin the mixture)
Makes 1 Large Serving

Nutrition: Suffice it to say that this one is out the roof with good for you nutrients, and its low fat.

In this chapter we learned a few more tips and tricks for customizing your Green Smoothies and experimenting with recipes. We even got a bonus Bloody Mary out of the deal!

In Chapter 11 we will learn the ins and outs of choosing and using a blender for Green Smoothies.

Choosing and Using a Blender

A blender is the only small appliance required for making smoothies. You can use the one you have or shop for one that is designed for making smoothies. Some of these blenders are very expensive and you should not run out and purchase a new one until you are sure that smoothie making is for you.

The number one requirement for a smoothie blender is the amount of power that it has. The more powerful the blender, the smoother the smoothie will be. The amount of liquid ingredients that you need to add when making a smoothie will depend on the power that the blender delivers.

The higher the power, the more liquid ingredients you will need. The high powered blender does a much more thorough job of liquefying the fruits and vegetables. Therefore, it will require more liquid ingredients to get the job done.

Less expensive blenders will require less or no liquid at all, but may leave you with a smoothie that is not as creamy as you would like. However, there are ways to get around this problem without investing in an expensive new blender. As we learned in Chapter 1, you have control over the ingredients in your smoothie and therefore, control over the results that you achieve. Here are the features to look for in a blender for making smoothies.

Power – You want as much power as you can get. It makes far less work for you. If you have a cheap blender with very little power, it will be difficult to get the smoothie consistency you are looking for without chopping, grating or mashing all of the ingredients in advance.

Tamping Tool – This handy tool comes with some blenders, and it allows you to push the ingredients down toward the blade and makes the whole process go a lot more smoothly. Making smoothies is a lot easier if your blender has this option.

Quality – You need a blender that does not have a plastic gear to turn the blade, they strip out too easy and then your blender is trash. Make sure the whole thing is sturdy and comes with a decent warranty.

You can purchase a blender for as little as $25 or spend over $1000. Let's compare our choices.

Inexpensive Blenders – We all know that we can get one cheap and it will work! However, there are several drawbacks to this option. On cheaper blenders, the gear that turns the blade is usually plastic and wears out very quickly. The longer you have to run a cheap blender, the more likely it is that the motor will burn up. So, if you have to replace it often to keep making smoothies, then you haven't really saved anything by going cheap. It also takes more time and prep work.

Mid-Range Blender – Blenders that run from about $200 to $500 are usually going to be more powerful and better built than the cheap blender. However, don't be fooled on the quality. Some in this range will be very good and some will simply be selling you a brand name that in the end will not deliver. Examine them carefully and go online and read reviews from other users before you choose one.

Expensive Blenders – These can range in price from $500 to well over $1000. Make sure you really are dedicated to making smoothies for the long haul, and that you really want to invest this much money in a blender before choosing this option. Sure, you will; get all the bells and whistles, but that won't matter if you don't use it.

If you decide to just use the old cheap blender you have for now, then prepare your ingredients and follow the 8 steps in Chapter 2 for making perfect smoothies.

Some of the expensive blenders today are designed to make perfect smoothies all by themselves, and they even have smoothie settings.

Mind you, I'm not knocking it, if it works for your wallet; but really, all of that is not necessary to make perfect smoothies!

In this chapter we learned what to look for in a blender and how much we can expect to pay.

In Chapter 12 we will discover a few more healthy tips to go along with our new Green Smoothie lifestyle!

Easy Tips for Excellent Health

There are no hard and fast rules that will insure that you achieve excellent health. Each and every person's body and their nutritional requirements are different.

I am a firm believer that life would be extremely boring if we were all just alike!

That being said, there are some basic principles that are necessary to the health of any human body. Experts have long tried to tell us that we need to eat X, Y and Z to be healthy. This is simply not true. What we need are the nutrients contained in X, Y and Z. There is more than one way to get those nutrients, and all of the nutrients we need are contained in far more than just one type of food. We can satisfy our taste buds and eat the foods that we prefer and be just as healthy as another person who eats entirely different foods.

If you are like me and have tried many approaches to your diet, you will realize, just as I did, that no two so-called experts can agree on anything about diet and nutrition. What is true today will be a big no-no tomorrow. The debates about carbohydrates, vegetarianism, raw foods, and the old standard five food groups, go on constantly. How do you decide what is right or wrong for you?

It is all about the nutrients. You need vitamins and minerals, good fats and protein among others. You do not have to eat meat to get your protein; other foods such as beans and greens offer comparable amounts of the proteins that your body needs. I am not advocating being a vegetarian; there is nothing wrong with eating meat. However, meat also adds a lot of fat to your diet that you don't need to consume all the time, just to get your protein. Here is a true story about my father that will illustrate my point.

My dad was a severe diabetic, taking insulin as much as three times a day. He had a very hard time following a diet that would help to control his blood sugar. (Meat fats are a major cause of high blood sugar.) His doctor told him to try eating beans; pinto, great northern, kidney beans, etc.; at least four or five days a week. When my dad followed this advice, he could eat whatever he wanted one day a week without it affecting his blood sugar. Low and behold, it had worked! My dad did love the all-you-can-eat-pork spareribs at the local barbeque joint on the weekend!

Regardless of the varying expert opinions on exactly which diet is the best and healthiest diet, all of them do agree on certain things. The body has certain fundamental needs in order to be healthy, and although most of these needs are food related, not all of them are contained in food. If you provide your body with what it needs, it will provide you with long years of healthy happy service.

Do not try to change your diet or your habits overnight. The body will not appreciate such sudden changes, and too many sudden changes, happening all at once, can have very unhappy consequences for the digestive system. It is best to add, or take away only one or two dietary changes at a time, until you strike a balance that works for you. *That is why adding a meal replacement Green Smoothie for breakfast or lunch is a great way to get started on a healthier you, without so much stress over it!*

Here are a few things that are absolutely necessary to the body.

Base your diet primarily on plant sources. Vegetables, fruits, nuts and whole grains are wonderful foods that provide most of the nutrition that your body needs.

If you eat meat, make sure it comes from grass-fed only farms. Processed meat has chemical additives, as well as water added to pump up the weight.

Avoid packaged foods at all costs. Manufactured snack foods, boxed dinners and dehydrated foods have had the nutrition processed right out of them. These foods and snack foods are mainly just empty calories that put excess weight on you.

Drink lots of water. Yes, I know that's what they all say, but it is true. Over 70% of your body is water. It has to be regularly replenished. It also flushes out your system and hydrates your skin.

Diet is not all there is to it! The human body needs exercise, sunshine and satisfying social interaction to be healthy. Don't deprive yourself of anything!

Most important of all is to remember that nothing happens overnight. It takes time to change a lifetime of habit. One or two things at a time are plenty and will make a difference that you can see. Pretty soon you'll be ready to make another change and another change!

Green Smoothie FAQs

#1 *Why should I put greens in my smoothie?*

If you don't, it won't be a Green Smoothie. You will also be missing out on all the nutrients that greens have to offer, some of which like Vitamin K are almost non-existent in other foods. Without the greens your smoothie will not be as filling or anywhere near as nutritious. Besides, you won't be able to taste them after you have added all of the other delicious ingredients in your smoothie!

#2 *What is actually meant by a bunch of greens?*

A bunch of greens is 4 to 5 cups of chopped greens. It does not necessarily correspond to the size of bunches in which you buy them, because different greens come in different sizes. You can also use bagged salad greens. If you reach and grab a large handful, it should come to approximately a cup when it is chopped. In Green Smoothies, the greens that you use do not have to be in exact measurements, a little more or a little less, really doesn't matter.

#3 *How long will my Green Smoothie keep in the refrigerator?*

A smoothie will keep however long the ingredients will keep. It is recommended not to keep them more than 24 hours, and for optimum flavor and nutrition you should drink them right away or at least within a few hours, say breakfast and lunch. As soon as the smoothie ingredients are processed and exposed to the air, oxidation begins and the nutrients begin to lose their potency.

#4 Are there any fruits and vegetables I should not mix together?

What ingredients you choose to use is strictly a matter for your own taste buds. This is an opportunity to try new things. The only thing you should be cautious about is using any fruit or vegetable that you know you have had an allergic reaction to in the past. Just replace those items in your recipe with something else. The only reason not to mix any fruit or vegetable, other than allergies, would be if it causes you to have digestive difficulties.

#5 What if I get tired or bored with Green Smoothies?

Try some new and exotic fruits or some vegetables you never thought to add. Go to the spice rack and pick out your favorite herbs, spices and extracts. Try them all with different food combinations. There are millions of ways to mix it up, so put on your thinking cap and soon you won't be bored with your Green Smoothie any longer!

In Conclusion

We have worked hard and we have learned much about Green Smoothies, and having a happy healthy body. *The fact is; it's easy and anybody can do it. No special equipment or appliances, no expert culinary skills required!*

Now we know that we can throw those old food groups out the window, because they really don't mean a thing. What matters is the nutrition you get from your food, and whether or not you are full and satisfied. It makes absolutely no difference what food those nutrients are in. You don't have to eat meat or dairy if you don't want to, and your bones and teeth are not going to fall apart.

You can get the same calcium, Vitamin D and protein from so many other foods. However, that option is always open. You may choose to use your Green Smoothies, for breakfast, a snack, lunch or whatever you choose and still eat any meal you choose any other time. Of course, the healthier those other meals are the sooner you will see the Green Smoothie benefits.

I am not here to preach a vegetarian diet or a raw food diet, or any other kind that would prevent you from enjoying a party or a holiday with your family. It's just that if you make a habit of **not** indulging in those types of foods every day, and adding that Green Smoothie to your diet, you will see and feel a major difference before long!

The truth is; if you replace one meal a day with a Green Smoothie, you will feel better, you will have more energy and maybe even lose a pound or two! That is a deal I can live with! How about you?

Fresh foods are just better for you all around than any processed pre-packaged food will ever be, no matter what they claim. And the truth is that fresh food in most cases is not as expensive as those popular products bearing expensive name brands. We all know about paying for name brands, now don't we? Why should we fill our bodies with all of those empty calories that cause our bodies to have to work too hard to get rid of, while they cloud our minds, and make us feel sluggish and tired? And forget losing any weight!

We have learned all the techniques we need to live happier, healthier, more well-balanced lives. We know it is possible to get rid of stress, boost our energy and immune system, and improve our hair and skin. What do we have to do to achieve all of this? Just have a simple and delicious Green Smoothie at least once a day, and more often if the mood and the desire strike us.

I cannot express to you what the Green Smoothie means to me. It has given me a new lease on life in my middle years, literally!

I may be over thirty, but I certainly don't feel it and I am quite sure that I no longer look like it. I am almost back to what I weighed in my 20s and 30s, and I am regaining my figure, as well.

I do exercise, however, I do it at my own pace and I do the things that I enjoy for my exercise. I don't have a regimen or plan, I just do something every day that uses different muscles and places me in different environments, so that I have a little variety. Most days, I don't even notice how much exercise I have actually done. I go for power walks in the park, I occasionally ride my bicycle, I do a little Tae Bo, I use a kettle ball some days and even sometimes jump rope. I swim when I can and I do simple leg exercises for horseback riding. It is not about working out, working out, working out; that is the surest way to get totally turned off by exercise in general, at least for me.

Your Green Smoothies are going to give you energy that you are going to want to use. Start out slow and take a stroll at lunch or in the evening. Take the stairs instead of an elevator whenever possible. Try parking farther away from where you are going, and walking in. Play with your dog or play with your children; throw a ball or a Frisbee in the park. Remember to have that Post Workout Green Smoothie to reboot your energy and replace the nutrients that you burn.

Never let yourself get dehydrated, drink lots of water, and I know that's what they all say! But, it is true. Your body is well over 70% water and must be constantly replenished. Without water, nothing in the body works right. That is why most Green Smoothie recipes incorporate some type of water or ice.

Green Smoothies offer a unique opportunity to incorporate many healthy nutrients that you may not normally be getting, simply because you do not like the foods that provide those particular nutrients. With smoothies, you can actually add highly nutritious vegetables and fruits to your diet and you won't even be able to taste them.

When you choose a smoothie for a meal replacement or snack, you will actually be saving yourself some time that you can spend doing something else that you enjoy! What better way to get complete and satisfying nutrition every day!